Original title:

Frosty Vessels Beyond the Elf Rill

Author: Linda Leevike

ISBN HARDBACK: 978-1-80559-235-8

ISBN PAPERBACK: 978-1-80559-734-6

Covert Mysteries Beneath the Frosted Canopy

Whispers echo in the night,
Shadows dance, just out of sight.
Beneath the frost, secrets creep,
Guardians of the woods, they sleep.

Moonlight weaves through branches bare,
Caressing dreams that float on air.
Each flake tells a tale untold,
Of hidden paths and stones of gold.

Crimson berries, bright and rare,
Linger softly, unaware.
Footsteps soft on snowy ground,
In the stillness, mysteries found.

Winter's breath, a gentle sigh,
Breathes life into the shrouded sky.
Nature's quilt, both warm and cold,
Cradles secrets, brave and bold.

Beneath the canopy so deep,
The world above, in silence, sleeps.
Yet in the frost, the stories lie,
Covert, waiting, to defy.

The Harvest of Dreams in Shimmering Snow

Glittering flakes fall from the sky,
Whispers of wishes as they sigh.
Each moment glows, a fleeting glance,
In this winter's wondrous dance.

Fields adorned in frosted white,
Hold the dreams of long-lost nights.
Silent echoes, soft and slow,
Gather secrets in the snow.

Nightingale's song, a lullaby,
Calls forth hopes that soar and fly.
Beneath the sky, stars brightly gleam,
As we gather the harvest of dreams.

Fires crackle, warmth ignites,
Filling hearts on chilly nights.
With every breath, we spin our fate,
In the magic we create.

So let us weave through winter's chill,
Embrace the dreams that time can't kill.
In shimmering snow, our hearts will glow,
As we dance through life, in ebb and flow.

Whispers of Winter's Embrace

Softly falls the gentle snow,
Creating peace where wild winds blow.
Trees adorned in silver lace,
Nature sleeps in winter's grace.

Silent nights with stars aglow,
Crisp, cold air begins to flow.
Footprints left in icy ground,
Echoes of a world unbound.

Fires crackle, shadows play,
Cozy hearts chase chill away.
Wrapped in warmth, the world stands still,
Winter's breath a soft goodwill.

Moonlight dances on the snow,
Casting dreams where night winds blow.
Whispers weave through frosty air,
Winter's voice is sweet and rare.

In this realm of white and gray,
Where time melts, and spirits sway.
Nature whispers, soft and mild,
In winter's arms, we are beguiled.

Silent Boats in Shimmering Crystals

Silent boats on frozen lakes,
Crystalline paths that nature makes.
Reflections shimmer in the night,
Guiding dreams with soft, pale light.

Gentle ripples fade away,
Echoes of a frosty play.
Misty breath in chilly air,
Binds the heart with tender care.

Moonlit sails of silver hue,
Drifting where the night winds blew.
Stars above in velvet deep,
Keep the secrets that they keep.

With each wave, a story told,
Of adventures brave and bold.
In the stillness, hopes arise,
Underneath the starry skies.

Silent boats in crystal grace,
Float within this tranquil space.
Time suspended, peace prevails,
In the hush where wonder sails.

Chilled Serenity on the Woodland Stream

Whispers glide on winter's stream,
Chilled serenity, a dream.
Branches arch in frozen hue,
Nature cradles all that's true.

Water dances, soft and clear,
Muffled sounds that seem to steer.
Quiet ripples trace the land,
In this stillness, peace we hand.

Pine trees stand in silent rows,
Guarding secrets nature knows.
Frosted leaves, a twinkling sight,
Glimmer softly in the light.

Woodland paths, a tranquil scene,
Embrace the cold, serene, pristine.
Every step a whisper shared,
In this quiet, all is bared.

Chilled serenity flows and glows,
Through the woods where stillness grows.
Nature's touch, profound and deep,
In the heart, these moments keep.

Glacial Dreams in the Frosted Vale

In the vale where shadows play,
Glacial dreams begin to sway.
Icy breath upon the air,
Crafts a world beyond compare.

Crystals hang from branches bare,
Draping nature with great care.
Silent winds in whispers share,
Stories woven, beyond glare.

Softly lands the winter's kiss,
Each flake a gentle wish.
Timeless patterns grace the ground,
In the stillness, peace is found.

Misty echoes, softly hum,
In this tranquility, we come.
Through the frost, life's beauty beams,
Carved in silence, glacial dreams.

In the night, the moonlight glows,
Bathing all the vale in prose.
Every corner holds a tale,
In glacial dreams, our hearts sail.

Fables of the Frost-Kissed Realm

In a realm where whispers freeze,
Stories linger in the breeze.
Frosty tales in silence told,
Echo beneath the stars of gold.

Mighty trees in white attire,
Guarding secrets in the fire.
Footsteps soft on glimmering snow,
Holding lore of long ago.

Crisp air hums with ancient song,
Calling spirits, brave and strong.
Icicles drip like frozen tears,
Woven deep with ancient fears.

Moonlight bathes the land in peace,
Where the chill of night won't cease.
Every flake a tale retold,
In the frost, their dreams unfold.

Now the night begins to break,
Painting dreams on porcelain lake.
Fables linger, time stands still,
In the frost-kissed realm, we thrill.

Elven Spirits Dancing in Crystal Clarity

Underneath the silver moon,
Elven spirits sway and croon.
In a dance of light and grace,
Shadows weave a tender space.

Glistening with morning dew,
Every step feels fresh and new.
Crystal clarity around,
Echoes of joy enchant the ground.

Their laughter fills the chilly air,
Magic sensed, both real and rare.
Whispers of the trees reply,
As stars above begin to sigh.

In the glade where silence reigns,
Every heartbeat softly chains.
Twirl and leap through night's embrace,
Caught in an ethereal race.

As dawn breaks the spell they weave,
In soft light, we learn to believe.
Elven spirits fade from sight,
Leaving traces in the night.

Where the Ice and Stars Converge

Beneath a sky of velvet night,
Where ice meets stars, a wondrous sight.
Crystalline paths glitter bright,
Guiding dreams with pure delight.

Frozen lakes like mirrors gleam,
Reflecting every whispered dream.
In this realm of cold and fire,
Hope ignites a fervent desire.

Winds carry tales from ages past,
Echoing memories that long last.
Each star a guide, a gentle nudge,
Where hearts can dance, and doubts can budge.

As frosty breath paints the air,
A moment's pause, a fleeting stare.
In the silence, secrets whirl,
Where ice and stars continually twirl.

When twilight falls, the magic sings,
Of the peace that winter brings.
In this land, forever merge,
Where the ice and stars converge.

Secrets of the Primaeval Snow

In the hush of winter's breath,
Lies the secret dance of death.
Primaeval snow drapes the land,
Whispers softly through the sand.

Layered deep, the memories lie,
Of ancients passing by the sky.
With each flake, a story spun,
Held in ice till time is done.

Crystals twinkle, soft and free,
Guardians of the history.
In their glimmer, truth unfolds,
Tales of warmth 'neath icy folds.

The echoes of a world erased,
In the snowy depth, embraced.
Silhouettes of life once known,
Speaking through the cold, alone.

As the sun begins to rise,
Awakening with morning sighs.
Secrets held in winter's glow,
In the beauty of primaeval snow.

Glittering Crystals on a Winter's Night

In the stillness of the night,
Crystals sparkle in the moonlight.
Whispers of frost kiss the ground,
Nature holds her breath, profound.

Trees dressed in shimmering white,
Glisten softly, pure and bright.
Stars above in quiet beams,
Casting light on chilly dreams.

Footsteps crunch on crisp, cold snow,
While the winter breezes blow.
Silence wraps the world in peace,
As all worries seem to cease.

Through the woods, a shadow glides,
Where the gentle hush abides.
Every glint a story told,
In this beauty pure and bold.

On this canvas, night draws near,
Filling hearts with quiet cheer.
Glittering crystals, pure delight,
Hold us close this winter night.

The Palette of Ice Adrift in Time

Frozen lakes, a painter's dream,
With colors swirling, a silent theme.
Blues and whites, a dance divine,
Nature's brush, the grand design.

Each shard of ice, a story spun,
From dawn's embrace to setting sun.
Echoes of seasons shift and sway,
In this frozen tableau, they play.

Glacial hues, reflections gleam,
Woven gently into a dream.
Time drifts lightly, soft and slow,
Whispers of magic, come and go.

As frost clings to the morning light,
Crystals shine, a breathtaking sight.
Nature's art, forever flows,
In the palette, beauty glows.

Through the vale and across the seas,
Ice will whisper in the breeze.
A tapestry of shadows cast,
A moment held, a memory vast.

Enchanted Drifts of Glacial Inspiration

Winds of winter sing their song,
As snowflakes dance the night along.
Drifts that sparkle, softly bright,
Crafting dreams with sheer delight.

Forests draped in icy lace,
Nature's art, a warming grace.
Whispers of the cold air weave,
Tales of hope, we dare believe.

Frosty branches, arching high,
Frame the canvas of the sky.
Between the shadows and the light,
Life finds joy in chilly bite.

Each moment wraps the heart in glow,
As enchanted breezes blow.
Inspiration from the cold,
Fills the soul as tales unfold.

Underneath the stars so clear,
Dreamers find they have no fear.
For in these drifts, one can see,
A world of wonder, wild and free.

The Nightingale's Lament in Frosted Woods

In frosted woods, the nightingale,
Sings a song of soft, sweet wail.
Notes that dance on winter's breath,
In the silence, echoes depth.

Beneath the branches, shadows weave,
Stories of those who thought to leave.
Yet the melody gently stays,
Filling hearts through chilly days.

Moonlit paths that twist and turn,
In every note, a flame does burn.
Nightingale, both brave and bold,
Tells of stories long untold.

Echoes lingers in the air,
Soft reminders of love and care.
With every chirp, a wish takes flight,
In the caress of winter's night.

As the woods wrap round so tight,
Holding dreams within their light.
The nightingale, a steadfast friend,
Sings of hope that will not end.

Reflections in the Quiet Ice

In stillness deep, the ice does gleam,
Mirrored skies in a frozen dream,
Whispers of frost on silent ground,
Nature's hush, a sacred sound.

Beneath the veil of winter's breath,
Life holds tightly, dances with death,
Fractured light in prismatic hues,
Awaiting spring, the heart renews.

Branches bare, yet strong they stand,
Guardians of this frozen land,
Glistening shards from heaven's tears,
Echoes lost through fleeting years.

Each crack and crevice tells a tale,
Of fleeting time, of dreams set sail,
In quiet moments, we embrace,
The beauty found in icy grace.

Ephemeral Beauty in the Winter's Hold

Frosted petals in morning light,
Glistening jewels, a pure delight,
Snowflakes dance on the gentle breeze,
Whispers soft through the shivering trees.

The world transformed by winter's sigh,
As shadows stretch and daylight's shy,
Each fleeting moment, a perfect frame,
Capturing winter's transient name.

Silence reigns in the snowy field,
Magic waits, our hearts to yield,
Underneath the cold, life stirs,
Hope entwined in whispered purrs.

As twilight falls, hues fade away,
Stars emerge, the night holds sway,
Ephemeral beauty wraps so tight,
In winter's arms, we find pure light.

Midnight Frost and the Wandering Oak

Under moonlight, frost does lay,
Crystals caught in a nighttime play,
The wandering oak, wise and grand,
Holds secrets of this frozen land.

Its branches twist, a story spun,
In slumber deep, the world is one,
Midnight whispers, cool and clear,
Dreams unveil when shadows near.

Beneath the stars, the magic calls,
As silence drapes and moonlight falls,
The oak stands firm, through storms and frost,
Guarding moments, never lost.

In the stillness, memories weave,
A tapestry, no hearts deceive,
Midnight frost, a gentle guise,
Where nature's spirit softly lies.

Elysian Landscapes of Frozen Wonder

Across the hills, the snowflakes spread,
Painting landscapes in purest bread,
Elysian dreams beneath the sky,
Where harmony and beauty lie.

Frozen rivers, a crystal flow,
Nature hummed in a winter show,
Whirls of white, a radiant crown,
Gentle whispers, soft and brown.

In valleys deep, the silence reigns,
With every breath, the stillness gains,
Impressions left by time's own thread,
As snowflakes drift, our hearts are fed.

A canvas vast, by moonlight kissed,
Elysian realms in winter's mist,
Each frozen moment, a timeless spell,
In the heart of winter, we dwell.

Crystalline Silences Beneath the Moonlight

In the quiet night so still,
Moonlight bathes the snowy hill,
Whispers dance on frosty air,
As dreams drift soft without a care.

Stars blink down with gentle grace,
Casting silver on this place,
Every shadow holds a sigh,
Beneath the vast, encircling sky.

Crystalline formations gleam,
Echoing a winter's dream,
Silent secrets softly told,
In the night's embrace, so bold.

Footsteps echo on the ground,
In the silence, peace is found,
Nature cradles all in bliss,
Underneath this moonlit kiss.

Hearts awaken with the dawn,
In the light, a world reborn,
Yet the silences remain,
Whispers of the night's refrain.

Wandering Spirits on a Frozen Tide

A frozen river winds its path,
Framed by trees in winter's wrath,
Wandering spirits softly glide,
Over ice, they dance and ride.

Mist rises from the water's face,
Whirling gently in a trace,
Echoes of a song long past,
Carried on the icy blast.

Ghostly figures roam the shore,
Memories of what was before,
In the stillness, shadows play,
Hushed as night turns into day.

Nature holds its breath in awe,
Embracing every silent flaw,
The world shimmers, cold and bright,
Wandering spirits take their flight.

Beneath the cosmos' endless dome,
In the frost, they find their home,
Cloaked in white, they intertwine,
On this frozen tide divine.

Shards of Light Between the Trees

In a forest, shadows blend,
Light through branches, softly lends,
Golden shards, like whispered dreams,
Dance along the sunlit beams.

Leaves shimmer, a tapestry,
Woven deep in harmony,
Nature's beauty all around,
In the silent, sacred ground.

Beams of sunlight filter through,
Creating magic, pure and new,
Every hue, a vivid show,
Color splashes, ebb and flow.

Beneath the canopy so green,
Life awakens, pure, serene,
A gentle breeze begins to weave,
Promise held in what we believe.

In this space where shadows play,
Light and dark both find their way,
Shards of brilliance in each sight,
Whisper secrets, pure delight.

Icicles Sing Beneath the Starlit Sky

Icicles dangle, crystal bright,
Catch the shimmer of the night,
Each one holds a song of cold,
Melodies of winter told.

Beneath a vast and twinkling dome,
Silent souls in nature's home,
Every star a guiding light,
As the world sleeps in the white.

Whispers rise from frozen ground,
In the stillness, peace is found,
Icicles hum in icy air,
Filling silence everywhere.

Moonbeams dance on snowflake's edge,
Nature's beauty, pure pledge,
Starlit sky, a shimmering sea,
Where dreams take flight, wild and free.

As dawn approaches, colors blend,
Songs of winter slowly end,
Yet the echoes softly ring,
In our hearts, the icicles sing.

Enchanted Currents of Icy Fantasies

Beneath the frost, a whisper sings,
Of snowflakes dancing on silver wings.
Crystals shimmer in pale moonlight,
While shadows play in the still of night.

A river flows, a ghostly stream,
Its icy surface, a winter dream.
Trees stand guard, their branches bare,
Embracing secrets in the cold, crisp air.

In twilight's grasp, reality bends,
As fantasy and truth are friends.
Echoes linger, soft and sweet,
In this realm where magic meets.

With frosty breath, we wander on,
Through tales of old and dreams long gone.
Each step a note in winter's song,
In enchanted currents, we belong.

Frost-kissed Reflections at Dawn's Break

Morning glimmers on frozen streams,
Awakening the world from dreams.
Golden rays touch the icy ground,
Creating splendor all around.

Frosty patterns glow with light,
An artist's touch in dawn's first sight.
Birds begin their gentle tune,
Heralding the sun's warm boon.

Whispers of winter fill the air,
As nature brushes without a care.
Reflections shine like polished glass,
In a fleeting moment, time will pass.

With every breath, a crystal sigh,
Dewdrops hang as the day draws nigh.
Underneath the waking sky,
On frost-kissed paths, we roam and fly.

Translucent Journeys Through the Snowy Hollow

Through silent woods, we softly tread,
Where fluffy drifts lie like a bed.
Sunlight filters, painting the snow,
In translucent shades that softly glow.

Footprints mark the winding way,
Leading us deeper; come what may.
Branches bend with every breeze,
Nature's whispers tease and please.

Time stands still in this hushed space,
As winter wraps us in its embrace.
A sparkling world of whites and blues,
In this hollow, we find our muse.

With each step, stories unfold,
Of ancient trees and legends told.
The heart of winter beats so slow,
In snowy hollows, we learn to glow.

Ethereal Echoes of the Winter's Flow

In twilight's hush, the echoes play,
Of winter's breath and fading day.
Ghostly winds weave through the trees,
Carrying secrets on the breeze.

Beneath a quilt of glistening snow,
Memories linger; soft and slow.
Frozen echoes, vast and wide,
In this ethereal winter tide.

The river murmurs tales untold,
Of ancient paths where hearts grew bold.
Each ripple sings a haunting song,
In the beauty of the cold, we belong.

Through forests deep and valleys wide,
Nature beckons; we glide and slide.
With hearts attuned to winter's grace,
In echoes, we find our rightful place.

Shimmering Silhouettes on Icy Winds

Whispers dance through the night air,
Shimmering shadows swift as flight.
Frosted breath on a silver chill,
Nature's canvas, a glistening sight.

Branches creak under icy spray,
Moonlight glows on the frozen ground.
Each silhouette tells a tale,
Of secrets lost and dreams unbound.

In the depths, the wild hearts roam,
Through the hush of the winter's song.
Ethereal forms in the moon's glow,
A fleeting glimpse, where souls belong.

Silent echoes of long-lost lore,
Crystals sparkle in the pale light.
Swaying gently with a soft breeze,
In the stillness, magic takes flight.

Underneath the starlit sky,
Lies a world where shadows play,
Shimmering silhouettes glide and spin,
On icy winds, they dance away.

Enchanted Frosts Beneath the Starlit Canopy

Underneath the velvet night,
Frosty whispers weave a dream.
Stars sprinkle tales of old,
In the hush, the silence gleams.

Gentle flakes fall from above,
Kissing petals, soft and light.
Each crystal, a story held,
In the depths of peaceful night.

Moonbeams waltz on frozen streams,
With a glow that's faintly bright.
Nature's magic cloaked in white,
Breathes enchantment, pure delight.

Shadows flicker, swirling round,
In the quiet, the magic grows.
Warmth of wonder fills the air,
As the galaxy softly glows.

Dancing fairies, pure and rare,
Whisper secrets on a breeze.
Enchanted frosts, beneath the stars,
Invite the heart to freeze.

Secrets of the Whispering Glade

In the depths of ancient woods,
Secrets linger, softly gleam.
Whispers rise from shaded glades,
Where the wild ones weave their dream.

Twilight veils the hidden paths,
Crickets hum, the night unfolds.
Moonlit streams of silver light,
Carry stories yet untold.

Leaves rustle with sacred lore,
Echoing the secrets shared.
The breeze carries sighs of souls,
Who sought peace and never dared.

Within each shadow, magic stirs,
Beneath the branches intertwined.
In the glade, the spirits dance,
With the echoes left behind.

Under the watch of timeless trees,
Whispers echo, fade away.
Every secret claimed by night,
Waits for dawn to greet the day.

The Frozen Currents of Twilight Tales

In the twilight, currents flow,
Frozen streams of silver grace.
Whirls of dreams in icy waltz,
Move with quiet, ethereal pace.

Misty veils wrap the landscape,
As shadows blend in soft embrace.
Each moment fleeting, hushed and sweet,
In the chill, time leaves no trace.

Candles flicker against the dusk,
Starlit whispers, a gentle song.
Currents of tales, both bold and shy,
Dance together, right and wrong.

Echoes of laughter haunt the night,
As frost enshrines the hearts of old.
Through the stillness, stories breathe,
Carried forth by voices bold.

Twilight holds a realm anew,
Where frozen tales weave and spin.
In each current, the past resides,
A tapestry, where dreams begin.

Moonlit Ice and Hidden Treasures

In the quiet glow of night,
Moonlight dances on the ice,
Hidden treasures gleam and shine,
Whispers of a world so nice.

Beneath the surface, secrets sleep,
Crystals form in jagged grace,
Echoes of a dream so deep,
Time stands still in this calm space.

Glistening paths of silver light,
Connect the realms of here and there,
With every step, the heart takes flight,
Beneath the stars, we breathe the air.

Frosted whispers fill the breeze,
Tales of wonder softly told,
In the night, the world at ease,
Embraced by winter, fierce and cold.

As dawn breaks with hues of gold,
The hidden treasures fade away,
Moonlit memories unfold,
A dance of night to greet the day.

Whirling Snowflakes on Elven Paths

Whirling snowflakes gently fall,
Across the elven paths they glide,
Softly weaving nature's thrall,
In a waltz where dreams abide.

By ancient trees, their branches sway,
Carrying whispers through the night,
In their arms, the snowflakes play,
A twinkling dance, pure and bright.

Elven voices hum a tune,
Intertwined with winter's breath,
Beneath the watchful silver moon,
Life's embrace defies all death.

Each crystal flake, a tale profound,
A journey through the cold and dark,
On elven paths, the magic found,
Illuminated by a spark.

With every step, the heartbeats meld,
In rhythm with the swirling snow,
In this realm where dreams compelled,
A love that only nature knows.

Crystal Heartbeats among the Frosted Pines

Beneath the boughs of frosted pines,
The crystal heartbeats softly play,
Nature's symphony intertwines,
With every breath, the night turns day.

Among the branches, whispers sound,
Harmonies of peace resound,
Each heartbeat echoes, nature-bound,
In this realm, tranquility found.

The snowflakes gently kiss the ground,
As shadows sway, a dance begins,
In the silence, magic found,
With every step, the heart still spins.

Stars above twinkle in delight,
Watching over this sacred place,
In the embrace of winter's night,
Time slows down, a sweet embrace.

As dawn approaches, gold will gleam,
Yet in this moment, all is pure,
The crystal heartbeats weave a dream,
A timeless bond that will endure.

The Allure of Winter's Embrace

In winter's grasp, a world transformed,
A blanket white, so pure and still,
With every flake, a dream is formed,
In silence, hearts begin to fill.

The allure of frost on every tree,
Whispers secrets in the air,
A kingdom carved in mystery,
Where magic dwells, beyond compare.

Footsteps soft on paths of white,
Each journey penned by nature's hand,
Carving stories in the night,
In a winter wonderland.

The warmth of breath in chilly air,
Brings promise of the sun's return,
In winter's hold, we find a layer,
Of beauty found within the churn.

As twilight glows, the stars awake,
And shadows dance on frozen ground,
In winter's arms, we find the break,
Where peace and love together sound.

Winter's Emissary Through the Twilit Glade

In shadows deep where silence dwells,
The silver moon casts frozen spells.
Through twisted trees in icy light,
The whispering winds take flight tonight.

A blanket white, where dreams entangle,
Footprints fade as night does dangle.
A breath of chill, the woods they sigh,
As winter's emissary roams nearby.

Glades adorned in crystal lace,
Each flake a gem, a fleeting grace.
With every step, the stillness grows,
In twilit realms where magic flows.

Echoes dance through frosted air,
Mysteries linger everywhere.
As nature sleeps in tranquil bliss,
A world transformed, a winter kiss.

In this embrace, I lose my way,
Among the shadows, night holds sway.
Yet in the dark, a spark ignites,
Winter's emissary brings the light.

Palaces of Ice on the Whispering Stream

By the stream where secrets flow,
Palaces rise with a glinting glow.
Ice-capped towers reflect the sky,
In the pulse of winter, dreams do lie.

The whispering currents tell their tale,
As frosted branches softly hail.
Through sparkling halls where echoes gleam,
Wonders crisp, as if in a dream.

Each crystal wall, a story spun,
In the heart of winter, all is one.
Frozen echoes, a serenade,
In palaces of ice, magic's made.

Gliding softly, the moon will grace,
The shimmering frost, a cold embrace.
Nature's beauty, so sublime,
Helps us pause and steal back time.

As dawn approaches, a gentle beam,
Melts away the night's cold dream.
Yet in my heart, forever stays,
The splendor of those icy days.

Luminous Silhouettes in Frosted Whispers

Amidst the stillness of the night,
Luminous silhouettes take flight.
Frosted whispers in the deep,
Secrets that the shadows keep.

Glistening forms dance in the glow,
With every breath, the magic grows.
Branches bent with dreams untold,
In the winter's grasp, behold the cold.

Softly glimmering, the stars above,
Twinkling down like scattered love.
A tapestry woven in chill and light,
Frosted whispers cloak the night.

Dimensions shift within the air,
Where time stands still with tender care.
Lost in wonder, we softly tread,
Through luminous paths where shadows led.

In the embrace of winter's charm,
Every heartbeat feels so warm.
Here in silence, the world feels right,
Luminous silhouettes in flight.

Enigma of the Glacial Horizon

Beyond the cliffs, the horizon glows,
An enigma wrapped in winter's prose.
Where ice meets sky in whispered tones,
A realm untouched, where time atones.

Cascading light through shards of glass,
Creates a mosaic where dreams amass.
In frozen stillness, secrets hide,
The pulse of nature, an ancient guide.

Each wave of frost, a tale unfolds,
Of battles fought and glories bold.
Whispers echo in the frigid air,
As mysteries linger everywhere.

With every breath, the magic swells,
In the heart of ice where wonder dwells.
The glacial horizon calls to me,
In its embrace, my spirit's free.

So I wander forth with open eyes,
To see the world in its frozen guise.
An enigma waits, both vast and wide,
In winter's realm, my heart will bide.

The Melody of Winter's Whispering Bow

In the quiet snowflakes drift,
Softly whispering to the night,
Branches bow with frosted gifts,
Nature's breath, an icy sprite.

Underneath a starry dome,
Echoes of the cold wind's song,
Frosted whispers find their home,
Winter's melody, pure and strong.

Silence wraps the world in white,
Secrets held in frozen grace,
Every shimmer, pure delight,
Time slows down in this sacred space.

Firelight flickers, shadows dance,
Hot cocoa warms the winter chill,
In this moment, hearts entrance,
Breathless beauty, peace instills.

As the moonlight gently glows,
Casting silver on the ground,
Winter holds us in its throes,
A tranquil hush, profound and sound.

Luminous Paths Through Frosted Enchantment

A crystal veil on every tree,
Paths ahead, a shining glow,
Footsteps soft, a reverie,
In the stillness, spirits flow.

Glistening under pale moonlight,
Every branch a magic wand,
Guiding dreams through the soft night,
In this wonder, we respond.

Frosted patterns, nature's art,
Whispers weave a tale anew,
Each step forward, warms the heart,
Awakens joy in skies so blue.

With every breath, the chill revives,
Laughter sparkles in the air,
Frozen moments, life survives,
In the silence, love laid bare.

Through the night, we shall explore,
Underneath the shining sky,
Frosted enchantments, we adore,
Hand in hand, you and I.

The Joys of Twilight in the Frozen Realm

Twilight paints the world in gold,
Frosted diamonds grace the ground,
Magic murmurs, tales retold,
In this realm, warmth can be found.

Shadows stretch and softly blend,
With every sigh, the stars appear,
Frozen whispers start to send,
Promises of warmth draw near.

Joy awakens with the dusk,
Every sparkle holds a dream,
In this twilight, hearts are husk,
Together, we create the theme.

Laughter echoes, pure and bright,
In the glow of winter's grace,
Moments shared, sweet as the night,
In each heartbeat, love we embrace.

As day fades and night takes reign,
Frosty breaths fill up the air,
In the stillness, free from pain,
The joys of twilight, sweet and rare.

The Sacred Stillness of Icy Waters

In the hush of icy streams,
Silence sings a sacred song,
Water glistens, holds our dreams,
Where the heart feels it belongs.

Fragile crystals float and play,
Reflecting light in soft refrains,
Stillness wraps the winter's day,
In the echo of our chains.

Frozen edges, timeless grace,
Nature whispers deep and low,
In this serene and sacred place,
Minds can wander, hearts can grow.

Around the edges, shadows trace,
Memories held in every fall,
In the water's pure embrace,
Peace descends on one and all.

As the twilight calls us near,
Icy waters, calm and bright,
In their stillness, we find cheer,
A sanctuary of pure light.

Enchanted Waters through the Frozen Woods

Beneath the trees so tall and grand,
Rivers weave a silken strand.
Whispers dance in icy air,
Magic woven everywhere.

Sparkling snowflakes gently fall,
Nature's wonders, a silent call.
Reflections shimmer, bright and clear,
Calling forth the heart to near.

Frozen paths where shadows creep,
Guarding secrets that they keep.
Echoes linger, soft and pale,
As we follow, we set sail.

Footsteps crunch on white-strewn ground,
In this forest, peace is found.
A symphony of chill embrace,
In this moment, time's slow pace.

With every breath, the world ignites,
Enchanted waters, soft delights.
Through frozen woods, we wander free,
Nature's heart, our melody.

Frozen Serenade at the Dusk of Magic

At dusk, the world adorned in white,
Stars awaken, bold and bright.
A serenade of winter's song,
In this moment, we belong.

Silence blankets all around,
In the stillness, magic found.
Moonlight dances on the frost,
Glories cherished, never lost.

Breath like fog in winter's air,
Time is paused; we know no care.
The horizon blurs with dreams,
As twilight paints the world in gleams.

Snowflakes swirl, a gentle waltz,
In this beauty, no one faults.
Through whispering pines, we glide,
Holding tight, hearts open wide.

At dusk, the magic softly sighs,
In frozen realms where wonder lies.
Together in this hushed embrace,
We find our home in winter's grace.

Shivering Pines Under a Celestial Gaze

Shivering pines in frosty air,
Bathed in starlight, pure and fair.
Whispers of the night unfold,
Stories that the trees have told.

Celestial gaze, a watchful light,
Guiding us through endless night.
Beneath the boughs, a world so vast,
In this moment, we are cast.

Softly crunching, footsteps sound,
In this wonder, peace is found.
A tapestry of dreams we weave,
In the stillness, we believe.

Cool winds sigh through branches tall,
Nature's magic keeps us enthralled.
Each breath a spark, each thought a dream,
In the starlit night, we gleam.

Shivering pines, our silent guides,
In their arms, our spirit hides.
Under celestial gaze, we roam,
Finding joy in night's sweet home.

The Mystique of Winter's Enchantment

In the mystique of winter's charm,
Nature wraps the world in calm.
Every flake a story spun,
In this season, we are one.

Haunting echoes of the past,
Moments frozen, memories cast.
A gentle touch of frost and sheen,
In this beauty, life is keen.

Winds whisper secrets soft and low,
In the quiet, feelings grow.
Amidst the silence, hearts ignite,
Warmth found in the chilly night.

Each dawn brings a new delight,
Underneath the frosty light.
Together, we chase shadows long,
In winter's grip, we find our song.

The mystique of this season's grace,
Leaves a fond and lasting trace.
In nature's arms, we find our way,
In winter's world, forever stay.

Glistening Paths in the Winter Fog

Through the mist, soft whispers creep,
Glistening paths where secrets sleep.
Footsteps echo, damp and clear,
In winter's arms, the world is near.

Frosty breath hangs in the air,
Nature cloaked in frosted care.
Silent trees bow low and slow,
In whispered tones, the cold winds blow.

Luminous lights twinkle bright,
Guiding hearts in silent night.
Every step feels like a dream,
In this fog, all things redeem.

Shadows dance with gentle grace,
Magic woven, time and space.
As the dawn begins to break,
Hope awakens, fears forsake.

Here in this enchanted land,
Winter's beauty, softly planned.
Glistening paths of purest white,
Lead us forth to morning's light.

Beyond the Crystal Edge of Time

Beyond the glass, where moments gleam,
Lies a world lost in a dream.
Fragments captured, soft and bright,
Whispers of a fading light.

Silent echoes, voices blend,
Each tick, a story without end.
Time unravels, threads unique,
In its dance, we find the meek.

Forgotten wishes drift on air,
Crystal visions, rare and fair.
Through the maze of what once was,
We seek truth in quiet cause.

Past and future intertwine,
In the space where hearts align.
Moments linger, softly cry,
In the calm, we learn to fly.

Beyond the edge, the shadows play,
Time's reflection, night and day.
In this realm, we seek our fate,
Beyond the crystal, love awaits.

Glittering Dreams in the Hushed Woodlands

In the forest, whispers sigh,
Underneath the starlit sky.
Glittering dreams take flight and soar,
Through the trees, forevermore.

Moonlight dances on the leaves,
As the night, its magic weaves.
Crickets play a gentle tune,
Beneath the watchful silver moon.

Hushed woodlands cradle hearts at rest,
In their bosom, we are blessed.
Every shadow tells a tale,
In the quiet, we set sail.

Night unfolds its velvet grace,
Guided by the forest's face.
Glittering dreams ignite the dark,
In the stillness, we find our spark.

With every breath, enchantment grows,
In the hush, where mystery flows.
Woodlands whisper, secrets deep,
In their embrace, our spirits leap.

A Dance of Shadows on the Still Waters

Moonlit ripples kiss the shore,
Shadows dance, forevermore.
Each wave curls, a soft embrace,
In this stillness, find your place.

Reflections flicker, dark and light,
Whispers weave through the night.
Crickets sing a lullaby,
As the stars begin to sigh.

Echoes of a world unseen,
In the twilight's gentle sheen.
Ripples rise, then fade away,
In the dance of night and day.

Shadows sway to secrets told,
In the silence, dreams unfold.
With every step upon the lake,
Life and love begin to wake.

Here where waters cradle fears,
We find solace, free from tears.
A dance of shadows, pure and bright,
Guides our hearts into the night.

The Chill of Solstice Dreams

In the stillness of the night,
The stars whisper secrets bright.
Silver shadows dance and weave,
In dreams where spirits softly cleave.

The moon hangs low, a guardian fair,
Casting light on winter's stare.
Frosty breath upon the air,
Stories told without a care.

Time stands still beneath the skies,
As echoes of the past arise.
Solstice magic fills the space,
Awakening forgotten grace.

With each breath, a world transforms,
In the heart of winter storms.
Chill of night, yet warmth within,
A tapestry of hope begins.

As dawn approaches, dreams take flight,
In the hush of fading night.
Solstice whispers in the breeze,
A promise held among the trees.

Enigmatic Frost Beneath the Ancient Boughs

Beneath the boughs of ancient trees,
Frosted whispers ride the breeze.
Mysteries shrouded in icy bloom,
Winter's breath dispels the gloom.

Crystals twinkle on the ground,
In the silence, secrets found.
With every step, the world awakes,
Through the mist, a path it makes.

Veiled in white, the woods do sleep,
In shadows, timeless stories creep.
Each branch bears tales of long ago,
Their echoes linger, soft and low.

Embers glow in the fading light,
Wrapped in layers of chilly night.
A dance of crystals, ethereal grace,
In this realm, we find our place.

Frozen beauty, an ancient song,
In nature's realm where we belong.
Beneath the frost, life waits and dreams,
In the heart of winter's schemes.

Starlit Whispers of the Winter's Veil

In the hush of falling snow,
Starlit whispers softly flow.
Veils of winter cloak the land,
A tranquil touch from nature's hand.

Underneath the glimmering sky,
The world seems to breathe a sigh.
Dreams unfold in shimmering light,
As shadows dance in gentle flight.

Every flake, a tale retold,
In the silence, secrets unfold.
Blanketed in starlit grace,
Time pausing in this sacred space.

With each breath of winter's air,
A fleeting moment, pure and rare.
Hearts alight with the moon's embrace,
As we wander through this serene place.

Whispers echo, soft and clear,
In the stillness, love draws near.
Starlit paths beneath the veil,
Guiding us where dreams prevail.

Glacial Petals and Frosted Ferns

In the garden of wintry dreams,
Glacial petals catch the beams.
Frosted ferns, a crystal sight,
Glistening under the pale moonlight.

Nature's artistry unfolds,
A tapestry of ice and gold.
Each branch adorned with frigid grace,
In this enchanted, frozen space.

Whispers of the chill surround,
In this magic, joy is found.
With every heartbeat, every breath,
A reminder of life's sweet depth.

Glacial blooms dance in the air,
Painting warmth with their cold glare.
Winter's kiss upon the earth,
Holds a promise of rebirth.

In the stillness, we shall see,
The dance of seasons, wild and free.
With glacial petals and frosted ferns,
The cycle of life forever turns.

Frolics in the Spellbound Frost

In the morning light, the snowflakes dance,
Children laugh, caught in a playful trance.
Footprints mark a trail in shimmering white,
Winter's chill, a crisp and pure delight.

Snowmen rise with smiles, wrapped in scarves,
Sleds slide down hills, echoing our laughs.
The world transformed, a magical scene,
Frolics abound in the frosty sheen.

Whispers of cold in the chill-laden air,
Nature's beauty, beyond compare.
Frost-kissed trees in silvery glow,
A winter wonderland, where dreams flow.

Through the snowy woods, the shadows play,
Curtains of frost, keeping warmth at bay.
With twinkles bright, the stars above,
An evening of magic, wrapped in love.

The Lure of Winter's Enigmatic Mirth

Under the pale moon, secrets unfold,
Stories of winter, timeless and old.
Crimson fires crackle, shadows flicker,
In this cozy warmth, moments grow thicker.

Sipping hot cocoa, a dash of cheer,
Winter's lullaby, soft in our ear.
Sprinkled with starlight, laughter resounds,
In the heart of the night, joy knows no bounds.

Mysterious frost, a delicate lace,
Whispers of winter in this quiet space.
Snowflakes like feathers drift from the sky,
Embraced by the magic, we let out a sigh.

Glistening nights cast spells all around,
In each frozen moment, wonders abound.
Letting go of time, wrapped in a dream,
Together we dance in the moon's silver beam.

Shimmering Memories on the Breath of Sirens

Echoes of laughter in the frosty air,
Gentle whispers linger, memories shared.
Chasing the shadows of moments long past,
Each breath a shimmer, a spell that will last.

Through hidden pathways, we wander with glee,
Unfolding the mysteries winter sets free.
Frost-kissed petals, each winged delight,
Guide us to realms where the stars are bright.

The breath of sirens calls soft from the glen,
In winter's embrace, we lose track of when.
Stories engraved in the lines of our hands,
Are whispered by snowflakes as time lovingly stands.

Wrapped in the silence, we hear the refrain,
The sweet song of winter, a soft, cherished pain.
Harmonies linger in heartbeats that pause,
Finding serenity in winter's warm cause.

Sapphire Echoes of the Winter Morn

A sapphire dawn breaks, the world gleams bright,
Whispers of winter dance with the light.
Each crystal shimmer, a story retold,
In the chill of the morn, new wonders unfold.

Gentle breezes brush through the frosty trees,
Nature awaking with a shiver, a tease.
Meadows adorned with a silvery hue,
A canvas of dreams, forever brand new.

Footprints trailing through mounds of fresh snow,
Echoes of laughter, the hearts all aglow.
Winter's caress in the soft morning air,
In each fleeting moment, we linger with care.

The sky's brushed in hues of lavender grey,
Time flows like crystals, so still on this day.
With sapphire echoes, we find our way home,
Into winter's embrace, forever we roam.

Ethereal Streams in the Heart of Winter

In the quiet woods, a whisper flows,
Beneath the cloak where the cold wind blows.
Nature's breath, a soft, frosty sigh,
Carving paths where the frozen dreams lie.

Icicles gleam with a silver gleam,
Reflecting the light, like a soft, gentle dream.
Branches bow low, kissed by the chill,
While silence wraps the world, a soft, sweet thrill.

Footprints linger, a story untold,
Of wanderers brave through the winter's hold.
Stars above twinkle, a celestial guide,
As heartbeats echo in the moonlight's stride.

Ethereal streams weave a tale of the night,
Where shimmers of frost twirl in dimmed light.
The spirit of winter, both fierce and fair,
Holds secrets of magic, floating through air.

So wander, dear soul, where the currents flow,
In the heart of winter, let your spirit grow.
Among the whispers and shadows that gleam,
Find solace and peace in the ethereal dream.

Celestial Frost and Elven Lore

In twilight's embrace, the frost starts to fall,
Whispers of elves weave a magical call.
Secrets entwined in the shimmering light,
Under the stars, in the depth of the night.

Wings of the nightingale gently take flight,
As silvered frost glistens, pure and bright.
Elven figments in laughter they dance,
In a world wrapped in frost, a mystical trance.

Circles of shadows beneath ancient trees,
Echo tales of ages carried by the breeze.
With each breath, the silence holds vast,
An elven story, from futures to past.

Moonlight illuminates paths of pure glass,
As celestial frost weaves a beautiful mass.
Each glimmering flake a tale to behold,
Of love and of light, in whispers retold.

Eternal the dance of the stars in the sky,
Guiding the lost as the moments drift by.
In the realm of the frost, find solace and core,
In the heart of the wood, discover the lore.

Echoes of Ice within the Hidden Grove

In the heart of the grove where shadows play,
Echoes of ice in the soft light sway.
Branches adorned with diamonds of white,
Illuminate stories that turn into night.

Whispers of secrets hidden from view,
Where frost-bitten petals kiss drops of dew.
A world softly wrapped in a crystalline quilt,
Where dreams intertwine and hopes are built.

Crisp air carries tales of ages old,
Of laughter and love in the mornings cold.
With every step, the ice begins to sing,
A melody soft, that the winter winds bring.

Glimmers of magic in every glance,
Leaves rustle softly, inviting a dance.
Among the stillness, the heartbeat flows,
In echoes of ice, the spirit knows.

So linger and listen, dear traveler true,
In the hidden grove where the cold winds blew.
Find warmth in the chill, let your heart be free,
In the echoing ice, let your spirit see.

Moonlit Reflections on Crystal Waters

By the river's edge, where the cool waters gleam,
Moonlight casts shadows like a delicate dream.
Ripples create patterns, soft and divine,
As stars align, in a celestial line.

Whispered secrets drift on a gentle breeze,
Carried by currents that flow with such ease.
The night wraps around, a blanket of peace,
With each heartbeat, let the worries cease.

Reflections shimmer, like hopes in the night,
Glimmers of silver, so pure and so bright.
The world stands still, within soft embrace,
The beauty of darkness in full, gentle grace.

Lunar glow dances on the water's skin,
As dreams wade through, where the heart can begin.
In this serene moment, the soul finds its tune,
In moonlit reflections, beneath the soft moon.

So wade deep into the depths of your heart,
Let the crystal waters play their part.
For in each reflection, a story unfolds,
A tale of the night, waiting to be told.

Echoed Lullabies of the Winter Woods

Whispers through the frosted trees,
Softly hum the evening breeze.
Crystals gleam in moonlit glow,
Nature sings, a song of slow.

Silent footsteps in the snow,
Echoed dreams of long ago.
Branches sway with dreamy sighs,
Winter's breath is lullabies.

Stars above like candles shine,
In the night, the world divine.
A symphony of soft retreat,
As slumber wraps the woodland neat.

Shadows dance beneath the light,
Crickets hush, and all is right.
The woods, they cradle every sound,
In this peace, all hearts are found.

Snowflakes twirl in silent flight,
Filling hearts with pure delight.
Each a wish, a whispered cheer,
In winter's arms, we hold them dear.

The Silent Dance of Snowflakes

Falling softly from the sky,
Snowflakes twirl as they drift by.
Whispers glide on winter air,
Every flake a dream to share.

Gentle patterns swirl and bend,
Nature's ballet never ends.
Laughter echoes in the cold,
Snowflakes shimmer, tales unfold.

Underneath the starry gleam,
They perform, the purest dream.
Glittering like diamonds bright,
In the hush of peaceful night.

Each one dances, unique grace,
Painting soft the world's embrace.
In their waltz, the world stands still,
Capturing our hearts at will.

And as dawn begins to break,
Glistening paths, the silence wakes.
Snowflakes whisper, time suspended,
In this dance, our joy is blended.

A Tapestry of Ice and Imagination

Frigid air, a canvas white,
Painting dreams in tranquil light.
Ice encrusted, trees adorned,
A world transformed, reborn, and worn.

Sparkling branches glint with joy,
Nature's magic to enjoy.
In the stillness, whispers weave,
Tales of wonder, dreams believe.

Reflection in the frozen streams,
Caught in time, the wildest dreams.
Fables written in the frost,
In each beauty, never lost.

Every flake a story spun,
In this realm, where hearts have run.
Imagination dances free,
Crafting worlds for you and me.

Underneath the sapphire skies,
Secrets wrapped in frosty ties.
A tapestry of glimmering grace,
In winter's hold, we find our place.

The Secrets Held in Winter's Grasp

In winter's hush, a secret sleeps,
Beneath the snow, a treasure keeps.
Frozen whispers, stories told,
In the shadows, dreams unfold.

Footprints mark where journeys start,
Every step a work of art.
In the silence, secrets grow,
Nature's heart begins to show.

Crystals shimmer in moonlight's gaze,
A soft glow in twilight's haze.
Through the bramble, hopes arise,
In every flake, a whispered prize.

Ancient trees, a watchful eye,
Guarding moments passing by.
With each breeze, a tale is spun,
Of winter nights and morning sun.

Snowy blankets, time is paused,
In winter's grip, we are because.
Holding secrets, pure and deep,
In the stillness, dreams we keep.

Celestial Ice Mirrors of the Forest

In shadows deep, where silence lies,
Reflecting dreams beneath the skies.
The trees wear coats of frosted white,
As whispers echo in the night.

Crystal shards on branches cling,
Nature's jewels, the cold winds sing.
Each glimmer caught in nature's breath,
Frosted beauty, a dance with death.

Through woodland paths, a secret glows,
A tapestry that winter sows.
With each step on the frozen ground,
Celestial peace, a soft surround.

Moonlit trails lead hearts to roam,
In icy realms, we find our home.
Mirrors of ice and starlit haze,
In the forest's charm, we lose our ways.

Amidst the stillness, magic stirs,
The ancient tales, our spirit whirs.
With every glance, the calm ignites,
In celestial mirrors, pure delights.

Whispers of Magic in Subzero Silence

In the breath of winter's chill,
Mysteries wake and hearts stand still.
Beneath the frost, the stories call,
In whispers soft, they touch us all.

Snowflakes fall like gentle sighs,
Painting dreams across the skies.
Each flurry holds a magic grace,
Subzero silence, a warm embrace.

Frosted breath, a dance in the air,
Secrets spun with a chilling flare.
Time slows down in this frozen haze,
Where night unveils its silvered ways.

Kindred spirits of winter's night,
Together bask in soft moonlight.
Carried forth on a winter breeze,
Whispers of magic set hearts at ease.

Though frigid winds may whisper fears,
Love transcends through icy tears.
In subzero calm, our souls align,
To chase the whispers, pure and divine.

The Dance of Snow upon Glistening Leaves

In tender grace, the snowflakes twirl,
A ballet where the soft winds whirl.
On leaves aglow, a pearl-white sheen,
Nature's canvas, a sparkling scene.

With each drift, the world transforms,
Embracing quiet, the heart performs.
Surrounded by winter's soft embrace,
The dance of snow, a timeless grace.

Glistening leaves hum their tunes,
Beneath the glow of silver moons.
In gentle rhythm, they sway and play,
While magic falls, the night turns day.

A shimmer of light on nature's art,
Breath of winter, a warming heart.
As seasons meld, the dance remains,
In harmony where love sustains.

So let us join in this snowy drift,
Embrace the beauty, a cherished gift.
For in the dance, our spirits fly,
On glistening leaves, beneath the sky.

Beneath the Winter's Canopy of Stars

Beneath the sky of velvet night,
Stars will shine with pure delight.
A canopy of dreams adorned,
In winter's grasp, we are reborn.

The world asleep, yet bright with light,
Whispers echoes in the night.
Snowflakes gather, a soft caress,
A tranquil hush, our thoughts confess.

Among the trees, the shadows dance,
In silver beams, we find our chance.
To wander free on paths of white,
Lost in wonder, hearts ignited.

A symphony of frost and glow,
Emotions shared in the softest flow.
While stars above begin to sing,
We find our truth, our souls take wing.

In winter's arms, we find our peace,
A moment cherished, love's release.
Beneath the stars, forever stay,
In winter's magic, night and day.

Nymphs of Ice Amidst Thawing Dreams

In twilight's glow, they dance and sway,
Nymphs of ice, in the light of day.
With breath of frost on winter's breath,
They weave their magic, shunning death.

Beneath the moon, in shadows deep,
They guard the secrets the night must keep.
With whispers soft, they call the dawn,
As dreams of spring begin to yawn.

Their laughter rings through frosty air,
In glistening realms beyond compare.
With every step, the snowflakes bloom,
A fleeting touch, dispelling gloom.

Yet time, it flows and won't abide,
As thawing dreams must choose to bide.
The nymphs retreat, their song a sigh,
In echoes sweet, they say goodbye.

Hidden Parables in the Frosted Glens

In glens where frost and shadows play,
Lie tales of old, wrapped in decay.
Among the pines, whispers entwine,
Hidden parables, ancient and divine.

Each flake that falls, a story spun,
Of battles fought, and victories won.
The chill of night holds wisdom deep,
In every drift, in secrets keep.

From whispered winds, the past awakes,
As quiet streams of silence break.
In frozen breath, the voices claim,
A chorus sung, without a name.

Beneath the ice, the earth rebirths,
Each frozen tale, measures worth.
In frosted glens, the truth reveals,
A timeless bond, the heart then heals.

Tales of Snow and the Elven Tribes

In forests deep where snowflakes fall,
Elven tribes heed winter's call.
With silver bows and eyes like stars,
They dance 'neath the moon, erasing scars.

In quiet strength, their stories weave,
Of love and loss, of hearts that grieve.
Through drifts of white, their laughter rings,
Among the trees, their spirit sings.

With every step upon the ground,
Echoes of ages lost are found.
In harmony, they live and thrive,
In tales of snow, the tribes survive.

Yet storms will rise, and darkness loom,
A test of hope, to face the gloom.
Together bound, they stand as one,
In the heart of winter, love's begun.

Captured Echoes among the Icy Valleys

In icy valleys, silence reigns,
Captured echoes whisper of chains.
Frostbitten breath hangs in the air,
Memories locked in winter's snare.

Among the peaks, where shadows glide,
The heart of winter must abide.
With snowy winds that sweep the night,
They carry tales of lost delight.

With each soft step on powdered ground,
A thousand voices swirl around.
Beneath the stars, the stories flow,
In icy mirrors, reflections glow.

Yet as the sun begins to rise,
The echoes fade, much to our sighs.
In fleeting time, the frost must part,
Yet still the whispers warm the heart.

Whispers of Icicles in the Moonlight

Beneath the silver glow at night,
Icicles hang, a shimmering sight.
They whisper secrets in the cold,
Of stories that the winter told.

The world is wrapped in frozen lace,
Each drop of light a fleeting trace.
The air is crisp, an ancient tune,
Echoing softly beneath the moon.

Shadows dance upon the ground,
Where silence weaves a spell profound.
Each breath a cloud, each heartbeat slow,
As time itself begins to flow.

In stillness, magic starts to weave,
As night embraces those who believe.
A fleeting warmth in the icy breath,
The whispers linger, defying death.

So let us wander, hand in hand,
Through frozen woods, a twilight land.
In the moonlight's crystal embrace,
We'll find our dreams in this cold space.

The Chilling Embrace of Winter's Lake

Ice blankets the shores, so serene,
A tranquil realm, a frosted queen.
The whispers of the lake so deep,
In winter's arms, the world falls asleep.

Reflections dance on a glassy face,
Chilling winds in a cold embrace.
Every ripple tells a tale,
Of journeys lost and ghosts that sail.

Beneath the surface, secrets lie,
Where shadows play and silence sighs.
A frozen world, both fierce and kind,
In winter's heart, the solace we find.

Crystal stars adorn the night,
As swans glide under soft moonlight.
Each breath a puff, each moment rare,
In winter's lake, we pause and stare.

So let us linger by this shore,
As nature whispers evermore.
In icy beauty, we shall stay,
Embraced by winter's cool ballet.

Elven Echoes in the Crystal Stream

In glades of emerald, whispers play,
The crystal stream shows joy today.
Elven voices, soft and light,
Sing to the stars, enchant the night.

Each pebble sparkles with magic's grace,
As water flows in a gentle race.
Reflections of dreams and tales untold,
In the heart of the forest, where legends unfold.

Moonlight blesses the flowing scene,
As shadows flit through the trees so green.
With every ripple, a story's spun,
In the elven realm, where time has run.

Nature hums a harmonious song,
In this sanctuary, where we belong.
Every echo, a heartbeat's reply,
As the stream carries whispers to the sky.

So let us wander, hearts set free,
In this enchanted land, you and me.
With every step, a spell we weave,
In the crystal stream, we'll always believe.

Glistening Reflections of Frosted Dreams

In dawn's embrace, the world awakes,
With glistening dreams, the silence breaks.
Frosted trees in a crystal coat,
Whisper whispers, like a lover's note.

Each branch adorned with icy lace,
Reflects the beauty of nature's grace.
Shimmering light dances on the ground,
In the frosted realm, such magic's found.

Clouds drift softly, a silver hue,
As morning's light paints everything new.
Every breath, a frosty sigh,
In dreams that linger, we learn to fly.

So let us tread on this icy floor,
With hearts aglow and spirits soar.
In the morning light, we shall partake,
In glistening reflections the frost does make.

Together we weave our stories bright,
In winter's embrace, bathed in light.
With dreams that sparkle, pure and true,
In glistening frost, found me and you.

Elven Shadows on the Frozen Shoreline

In twilight's glow, they dance and play,
Beneath the stars, where snowflakes sway.
Whispers of magic weave through the night,
Elven shadows in the soft moonlight.

Their laughter echoes on the frosty breeze,
While silver waves caress the frozen trees.
Footprints silken on the powdery snow,
In this enchanted world, they ebb and flow.

With eyes like gems, they gaze afar,
At the shimmering sea and the evening star.
Forever bound to the winter's grace,
Elven shadows in this timeless place.

Through crystal forests, they weave and glide,
In harmony with nature, side by side.
With every flicker, the night confirms,
That magic lives in their graceful terms.

As dawn approaches, they fade from sight,
Leaving behind a dream of light.
But in the heart, their song will stay,
Elven shadows to guide the way.

Glacial Murmurs of the Ancient River

Beneath the ice, the river flows,
Whispers of time where silence grows.
Glacial murmurs, secrets untold,
Of ancient paths and stories bold.

In winter's grip, the water sings,
Of mountain peaks and winter kings.
Each ripple tells of journeys past,
Through frozen dreams, their shadows cast.

The banks are dressed in purest white,
While stars reflect in the quiet night.
Flowing softly, a gentle sigh,
As echoes of history drift on high.

With every current, whispers rise,
Of winter's chill beneath the skies.
The river knows the tales of yore,
Of glacial murmurs forevermore.

Time folds gently, on crystal waves,
Through silent caverns, the river paves.
An ancient song in winter's breath,
Carried softly through life and death.

The Braids of Ice in Nature's Dream

In nature's dream, the ice entwines,
Like ribbons spun in delicate lines.
A tapestry of frost, so fine,
Braids of ice where the sun doth shine.

Each crystal branch, a story told,
In shimmering patterns of silver and gold.
Nature's brush paints with gentle care,
The beauty rests in the winter air.

The frozen streams weave in and out,
With secrets shared, they whisper about.
Life's rhythm slows in the chilly haze,
Lost in the wonder of wintered days.

As shadows stretch and daylight fades,
The braids of ice in twilight cascades.
A moment captured in time's embrace,
In nature's dream, a tranquil space.

Awakened softly by morning light,
The ice glimmers with a touch so bright.
Each breath a cloud in the crisp air,
In nature's dream, peace settles there.

Winter's Breath on the Riverbank

Along the riverbank, winter sighs,
With breath so cold, it paints the skies.
Frost-kissed reeds bend with the breeze,
Whispers of chill among the trees.

The water flows, but ice frames the edge,
A glistening border, nature's pledge.
Beneath the surface, life pulses deep,
While snowflakes dance, sweet secrets keep.

In silence wrapped, the world stands still,
Winter's breath echoes on the hill.
The moonlight glows on the frozen span,
A silver pathway 'neath stars that ran.

Frosty tendrils grasp at the night,
As shadows stretch in pale moonlight.
With every heartbeat of the earth,
Winter's breath whispers of rebirth.

And when the dawn breaks crisp and clear,
The river hums, inviting near.
With every ripple, warmth will return,
For winter's breath, each heart will yearn.